All about Bats

by Bibi Boynton

A bat is a mammal. It is the only mammal that can fly. A bat can fly high in the sky. It can fly fast too.

Bats are not all the same size. Some may be big. Others may be small. One kind of bat is as small as a bee!

Bats have two legs, two feet, and ten fingers. Some bats have big ears, and some have small ears. All bats have fur.

Many bats live in caves, far away from the light. Bats sleep mostly in the daytime. They sleep upside down.

Bats can see very well in the dark. They hunt for food at night. A bat is awake while you are asleep.

Some bats eat fruit. The bats drop the seeds as they fly. The seeds land on the soil. New fruit trees will grow from these seeds.

When some bats find bugs, the bats eat them. A bat can eat 600 bugs in one hour. Those bugs will not bug you. So, you see, bats help us a lot.

Essential Vocabulary

Phonics Words Introduced
be, bee, bug(s), daytime, find, fly, high, kind, light, night, size, sky, too, two, upside, while

Vocabulary Words
bat, caves, fingers, fly, fur, hour, mammal

Sight Words
a, all, are, as, at, away, be, big, can, down, eat, find, for, from, have, help, here, in, is, it, many, may, new, not, of, on, one, only, other(s), see, so, some, that, the, them, these, they, too, two, us, very, well, when, will, you

Many people are afraid of bats. Some people think they are just rats with wings. But they aren't rodents. Bats are actually mammals! In **All About Bats** you will practice your phonics skills while learning about the interesting world of bats.